On Christmas Day in the Morning!

ON CHRISTMAS DAY

CAROLS GATHERED BY JOHN LANGSTAFF

PIANO SETTINGS BY MARSHALL WOODBRIDGE

IN THE MORNING!

ILLUSTRATED BY ANTONY GROVES-RAINES

HARCOURT, BRACE AND COMPANY, NEW YORK

*For my mother and father
who gave us, as little children, the joys
of singing Christmas music together as a family*

ERE are some traditional Christmas carols that can be enjoyed by all the family. They came from across the ocean hundreds of years ago and have been sung in families here ever since. They were not written by one person but sung by grandmothers and grandfathers, and mothers and fathers to their children, and learned and passed on that way. So they belong to all of us, like the other story-songs that we call folk songs and ballads. People sing these carols differently in lots of places, and what I have done is to choose the verses I like best from different parts of the world.

A carol is not just a Christmas hymn. It is much more exciting, because it can be a dance too! In our family, when the children sing "Dame Get Up and Bake Your Pies," we all hold hands in a circle and dance around, acting out verses and making up our own singing game. "I Saw Three Ships" is a gay folk-dance tune, which is still danced as a processional in Cornwall, and its infectious rhythm lifts a child into a natural jig. "There Was a Pig Went Out to Dig" must have been a mummers' carol generations ago, and it is still picked up quickly by children to act out or pantomime in some simple way. When my daughter was three years old, she added her own words and sang, "There was a *worm* went out to *squirm* on Chris-i-mas Day in the morning." For nearly eight hundred years, "The Friendly Beasts" has been sung and acted out; and in France, they used to ride a real donkey into church while they sang the medieval tune this way:

Many Christmas songs are about animals. They were at the manger when Jesus was born; and many people have thought ever since that, on Christmas Eve at midnight, all the animals speak again and kneel to praise the Child! J.L.

On Chris-i-mas Day in the Morning

There was a Pig went out to dig,
    Chris-i-mas Day, Chris-i-mas Day.
There was a Pig went out to dig
    On Chris-i-mas Day in the morning!

There was a Cow went out to plough,
Chris-i-mas Day, Chris-i-mas Day.
There was a Cow went out to plough
On Chris-i-mas Day in the morning!

There was a Sparrow went out to harrow,
Chris-i-mas Day, Chris-i-mas Day.
There was a Sparrow went out to harrow
On Chris-i-mas Day in the morning!

There was a Crow went out to sow,
Chris-i-mas Day, Chris-i-mas Day.
There was a Crow went out to sow
On Chris-i-mas Day in the morning!

There was a Sheep went out to reap,
    Chris-i-mas Day, Chris-i-mas Day.
There was a Sheep went out to reap
    On Chris-i-mas Day in the morning!

There was a Drake went out to rake,
    Chris-i-mas Day, Chris-i-mas Day.
There was a Drake went out to rake
    On Chris-i-mas Day in the morning!

There was a Minnow went out to winnow,
Chris-i-mas Day, Chris-i-mas Day.
There was a Minnow went out to winnow
On Chris-i-mas Day in the morning!

On Chris-i-mas Day in the Morning

There was a Pig went out to dig, Chris - i - mas Day,

Chris - i - mas Day. There was a Pig went out to dig On

Chris - i - mas Day in the morn - ing!

There was a Cow went out to plough,
Chris-i-mas Day, Chris-i-mas Day.
There was a Cow went out to plough
On Chris-i-mas Day in the morning!

There was a Sparrow went out to harrow,
Chris-i-mas Day, Chris-i-mas Day.
There was a Sparrow went out to harrow
On Chris-i-mas Day in the morning!

There was a Crow went out to sow,
   Chris-i-mas Day, Chris-i-mas Day.
There was a Crow went out to sow
   On Chris-i-mas Day in the morning!

There was a Sheep went out to reap,
   Chris-i-mas Day, Chris-i-mas Day.
There was a Sheep went out to reap
   On Chris-i-mas Day in the morning!

There was a Drake went out to rake,
   Chris-i-mas Day, Chris-i-mas Day.
There was a Drake went out to rake
   On Chris-i-mas Day in the morning!

There was a Minnow went out to winnow,
   Chris-i-mas Day, Chris-i-mas Day.
There was a Minnow went out to winnow
   On Chris-i-mas Day in the morning!

Dame, Get Up and Bake Your Pies

Dame, get up and bake your pies,
   bake your pies, bake your pies.
Dame, get up and bake your pies
   on Christmas Day in the morning!

Dame, what makes your ducks to cry,
    ducks to cry, ducks to cry?
Dame, what makes your ducks to cry
    on Christmas Day in the morning?

Their wings are cut, they cannot fly,
    cannot fly, cannot fly.
Their wings are cut, they cannot fly
    On Christmas Day in the morning!

Dame, what makes your maidens lie,
    maidens lie, maidens lie?
Dame, what makes your maidens lie
    on Christmas Day in the morning?

Dame, get up and bake your pies,
    bake your pies, bake your pies.
Dame, get up and bake your pies
    on Christmas Day in the morning!

Dame, Get Up and Bake Your Pies

Dame, get up and bake your pies, bake your pies, bake your pies.

Dame, get up and bake your pies— on Christmas Day in the morning!

Dame, what makes your ducks to cry,
  ducks to cry, ducks to cry?
Dame, what makes your ducks to cry
  on Christmas Day in the morning?

Their wings are cut, they cannot fly,
  cannot fly, cannot fly.
Their wings are cut, they cannot fly
  On Christmas Day in the morning!

Dame, what makes your maidens lie,
  maidens lie, maidens lie?
Dame, what makes your maidens lie
  on Christmas Day in the morning?

Dame, get up and bake your pies,
  bake your pies, bake your pies.
Dame, get up and bake your pies
  on Christmas Day in the morning!

I Saw Three Ships

I saw three ships come sailing in
> On Christmas Day, on Christmas Day.
I saw three ships come sailing in
> On Christmas Day in the morning.

And who was in those ships all three
> On Christmas Day, on Christmas Day?
And who was in those ships all three
> On Christmas Day in the morning?

'Twas Joseph and his Fair Ladye
      On Christmas Day, on Christmas Day.
'Twas Joseph and his Fair Ladye
      On Christmas Day in the morning.

O, he did whistle and she did sing
      On Christmas Day, on Christmas Day.
O, he did whistle and she did sing
      On Christmas Day in the morning!

Saint Michael was the steerés-man
    On Christmas Day, on Christmas Day.
Saint Michael was the steerés-man
    On Christmas Day in the morning.

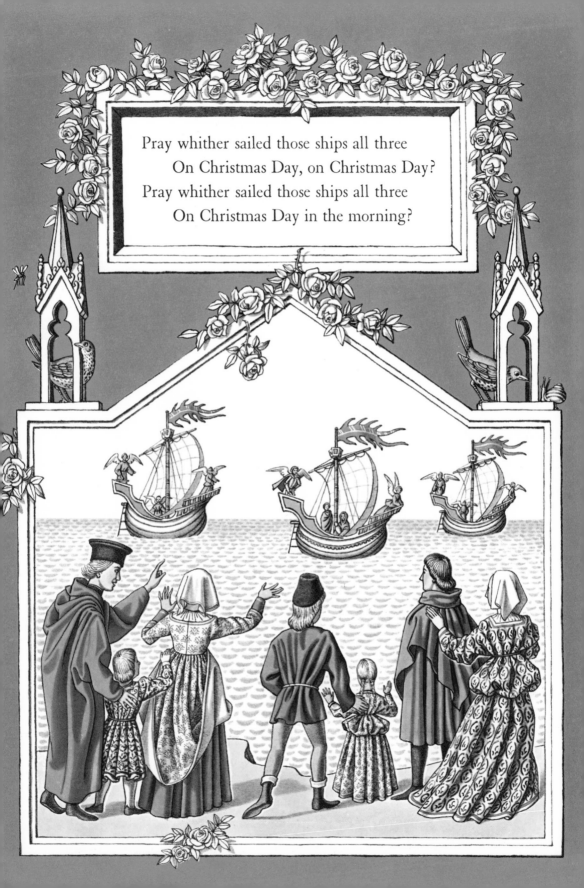

Pray whither sailed those ships all three
On Christmas Day, on Christmas Day?
Pray whither sailed those ships all three
On Christmas Day in the morning?

O, they sailed into Bethlehem
    On Christmas Day, on Christmas Day.
O, they sailed into Bethlehem
    On Christmas Day in the morning!

And all the bells on earth shall ring
On Christmas Day, on Christmas Day.
And all the bells on earth shall ring
On Christmas Day in the morning!

I Saw Three Ships

I saw three ships come sailing in On Christmas Day, on Christmas Day. I saw three ships come sailing in On Christmas Day in the morning. And who was in those ships all three On Christmas Day, on Christmas Day? And who was in those ships all three On

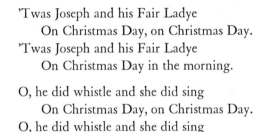

Christ - mas   Day ___   in   the   morn -   ing?

'Twas Joseph and his Fair Ladye
    On Christmas Day, on Christmas Day.
'Twas Joseph and his Fair Ladye
    On Christmas Day in the morning.

O, he did whistle and she did sing
    On Christmas Day, on Christmas Day.
O, he did whistle and she did sing
    On Christmas Day in the morning!

Saint Michael was the steerés-man
    On Christmas Day, on Christmas Day.
Saint Michael was the steerés-man
    On Christmas Day in the morning.

Pray whither sailed those ships all three
    On Christmas Day, on Christmas Day?
Pray whither sailed those ships all three
    On Christmas Day in the morning?

O, they sailed into Bethlehem
    On Christmas Day, on Christmas Day.
O, they sailed into Bethlehem
    On Christmas Day in the morning!

And all the bells on earth shall ring
    On Christmas Day, on Christmas Day.
And all the bells on earth shall ring
    On Christmas Day in the morning!

The Friendly Beasts

Jesus, our brother, kind and good,
    Was humbly born in a stable rude;
And the friendly beasts around Him stood.
    Jesus, our brother, kind and good.

"I," said the Donkey, shaggy and brown,
    "I carried His mother up hill and down;
I carried His mother to Bethlehem town."
    "I," said the Donkey, shaggy and brown.

"I," said the Cow, all white and red,
　　"I gave Him my manger for His bed;
I gave Him my hay to pillow His head."
　　"I," said the Cow, all white and red.

"I," said the Sheep, with the curly horn,
    "I gave Him my wool for His blanket warm;
He wore my coat on Christmas morn."
    "I," said the Sheep, with the curly horn.

"I," said the Dove, from the rafters high,
    "Cooed Him to sleep that He should not cry;
We cooed Him to sleep, my mate and I."
    "I," said the Dove, from the rafters high.

Thus every beast by some glad spell,
In the stable dark was glad to tell
Of the gift he gave Emmanuel,
The gift he gave Emmanuel.

The Friendly Beasts

Je - sus, our broth - er, kind and good, Was hum - bly born in a sta - ble rude; And the friend - ly beasts a - round Him stood. Je - sus, our broth - er, kind and good.

"I," said the Donkey, shaggy and brown,
"I carried His mother up hill and down;
I carried His mother to Bethlehem town."
"I," said the Donkey, shaggy and brown.

"I," said the Cow, all white and red,
"I gave Him my manger for His bed;
I gave Him my hay to pillow His head."
"I," said the Cow, all white and red.

"I," said the Sheep, with the curly horn,
    "I gave Him my wool for His blanket warm;
He wore my coat on Christmas morn."
    "I," said the Sheep, with the curly horn.

"I," said the Dove, from the rafters high,
    "Cooed Him to sleep that He should not cry;
We cooed Him to sleep, my mate and I."
    "I," said the Dove, from the rafters high.

Thus every beast by some glad spell,
    In the stable dark was glad to tell
Of the gift he gave Emmanuel,
    The gift he gave Emmanuel.